EASY STUDIES Vol. I

by Ch. Dancla, H. E. Kayser, H. Sitt and F. Wohlfahrt
for Violin and Orchestra

(1st Position)

Piano Reduction by
Gero Stöver

DOWANI International

Contents / Contenu / Inhalt

Preface

With this volume we are pleased to offer you something entirely new in the field of violin teaching: the premiere publication of well-known violin studies by Charles Dancla, Heinrich Ernst Kayser, Hans Sitt and Franz Wohlfahrt with *orchestral accompaniment.* The aim of these practical edition is to give all violinists the impetus and motivation they need to practice studies on a daily basis.

Practicing studies is a very important part of the training of every music student, learner, amateur and professional. These newly arranged orchestral accompaniments to well-known studies give rise to miniature violin concertos, thereby turning the practicing of studies into an entirely new experience and a source of enjoyment, especially for beginners.

The orchestral arrangements and piano reductions are the work of Gero Stöver, who has masterfully combined subtle orchestral timbres with the rather simple harmonies of the studies. The pieces are relatively easy to play, lying within the first position. This allows you to focus entirely on the music and to hear and grasp it consciously. *DOWANI 3 Tempi Play Along* offers you an ideal starting point for this.

The CD opens with the concert version of each study, that is, the violin part with orchestral accompaniment. After tuning your instrument (Track 1), the musical work can begin. Your first practice session should be at slow tempo. If your stereo system is equipped with a balance control, you can place either the violin or the piano accompaniment in the foreground by adjusting the control. The violin always remains softly audible in the background as a guide. In the middle position, both instruments can be heard at the same volume. If you do not have a balance control, you can listen to the solo part on one loudspeaker and the piano part on the other. Having mastered the slow tempo, you can now advance to the medium and original tempos. The piano or orchestral accompaniment can be heard on both channels (without violin) in stereo quality. The studies have been sensibly divided into subsections for practice purposes. You can select the subsection you want using the track numbers indicated in the solo part. Further explanations can be found at the end of this volume along with the names of the musicians involved in the recording. More detailed information can be found on the internet at www.dowani.com. All of the pieces were recorded live.

To shorten the distance from the CD to the experience of live music-making, we offer all orchestras a complete set of performance material, including a conductor's score.

We wish you lots of fun playing from our *DOWANI 3 Tempi Play Along* editions and hope that your musicality and diligence will enable you to play the concert version as soon as possible. Our goal is to provide the essential conditions you need for effective practicing through motivation, enjoyment and fun.

Your DOWANI Team

Avant-propos

Nous sommes heureux de pouvoir vous présenter avec ce recueil une nouveauté mondiale dans le domaine de la pédagogie instrumentale pour violon : la première édition d'un recueil d'études connues pour violon de Charles Dancla, Heinrich Ernst Kayser, Hans Sitt et Franz Wohlfahrt avec *accompagnement d'orchestre.* Nous souhaitons donner avec cette édition pratique une impulsion et une motivation nouvelles à tous les violonistes pour l'exercice quotidien des études.

Le travail des études est un élément très important dans la formation musicale de chaque élève, étudiant, amateur et pianiste professionnel. Avec de nouveaux arrangements pour accompagnement d'orchestre, les études connues ressemblent à des concertos pour violon en miniature. Ainsi le travail des études deviendra une expérience d'un type nouveau qui apportera aussi beaucoup de plaisir aux débutants.

Les arrangements orchestraux et les réductions pour piano ont été réalisés par Gero Stöver qui sait très bien lier des images sonores subtiles et des grands mouvements d'orchestre aux structures harmoniques relativement faciles des études. Le degré de difficulté des morceaux choisis se situe dans la catégorie "facile" (1ère position). Vous pourrez ainsi vous concentrer entièrement sur la musique pour bien l'écouter et la comprendre. La collection *DOWANI 3 Tempi Play Along* constitue pour cela un point de départ idéal.

Le CD vous permettra d'entendre d'abord la version de concert de chaque morceau (violon avec accompagnement d'orchestre). Après avoir accordé votre instrument (plage N°1), vous pouvez commencer le travail musical. Votre premier contact avec les morceaux devrait se faire à un tempo lent. Si votre chaîne hi-fi dispose d'un réglage de balance, vous pouvez l'utiliser pour mettre au premier plan soit le violon, soit l'accompagnement de piano. Le violon restera cependant toujours très doucement à l'arrière-plan comme point de repère. En équilibrant la balance, vous entendrez les deux instruments à volume égal. Si vous ne disposez pas de réglage de balance, vous entendrez l'instrument soliste sur un des haut-parleurs et le piano sur l'autre. Après avoir étudié le morceau à un tempo lent, vous pourrez ensuite travailler à un tempo modéré et au tempo original. Dans ces deux tempos vous entendrez l'accompagnement de piano ou d'orchestre sur les deux canaux en stéréo (sans la partie soliste). De plus, les études ont été judicieusement divisées en plusieurs passages à travailler. Vous pouvez sélectionner ces passages à l'aide des numéros de plages indiqués dans la partie du soliste. Pour obtenir plus d'informations et les noms des artistes qui ont participé aux enregistrements, veuillez consulter la dernière page de cette édition ou notre site Internet : www.dowani.com. Toutes les versions ont été enregistrées en direct.

Pour que le pas entre le CD et le concert ne soit pas trop long à franchir, nous proposons à tous les orchestres le matériel d'orchestre avec conducteur.

Nous vous souhaitons beaucoup de plaisir à faire de la musique avec la collection *DOWANI 3 Tempi Play Along* et nous espérons que votre musicalité et votre application vous amèneront aussi rapidement que possible à la version de concert. Notre but est de vous offrir les bases nécessaires pour un travail efficace par la motivation et le plaisir.

Les Éditions DOWANI

Vorwort

Wir freuen uns, Ihnen mit dieser Ausgabe eine Weltneuheit auf dem Gebiet der Violinpädagogik vorstellen zu können: die erste Ausgabe bekannter Violinetüden von Charles Dancla, Heinrich Ernst Kayser, Hans Sitt und Franz Wohlfahrt mit *Orchesterbegleitung*. Mit dieser praxisorientierten Ausgabe möchten wir allen Geigern neue Impulse und Motivationserlebnisse für das tägliche Üben von Etüden geben.

Das Üben von Etüden ist ein sehr wichtiger Bestandteil der Musikerziehung eines jedes Musikschülers, Studenten, Amateurs oder Profis. Die neu arrangierten Orchesterbegleitungen zu bekannten Etüden lassen Violinkonzerte im Miniaturstil entstehen. Dadurch wird das Üben von Etüden zu einem ganz neuen Erlebnis und bereitet vor allem auch Anfängern große Freude.

Die Orchesterarrangements und Klavierauszüge stammen von Gero Stöver, der es ausgezeichnet versteht, subtile Klangmalereien sowie ausladende Orchestersätze mit den harmonisch eher einfacheren Strukturen der Etüden zu verbinden. Der Schwierigkeitsgrad dieser Stücke liegt im leichten Bereich (1. Lage). Somit können Sie sich ganz auf die Musik konzentrieren und sie bewusst hören und verstehen. Dafür bietet Ihnen *DOWANI 3 Tempi Play Along* eine optimale Ausgangsbasis.

Auf der CD können Sie zuerst die Konzertversion eines jeden Stückes (Violine mit Orchesterbegleitung) anhören. Nach dem Stimmen Ihres Instrumentes (Track 1) kann die musikalische Arbeit beginnen. Ihr erster Übe-Kontakt mit den Stücken sollte im langsamen Tempo stattfinden. Wenn Ihre Stereoanlage über einen Balance-Regler verfügt, können Sie durch Drehen des Reglers entweder die Violine oder die Klavierbegleitung stufenlos in den Vordergrund blenden. Die Violine bleibt jedoch immer als Orientierungshilfe – wenn auch sehr leise – hörbar. In der Mittelposition erklingen beide Instrumente gleich laut. Falls Sie keinen Balance-Regler haben, hören Sie das Soloinstrument auf dem einen Lautsprecher, das Klavier auf dem anderen. Nachdem Sie das Stück im langsamen Tempo einstudiert haben, können Sie im mittelschnellen und originalen Tempo musizieren. Die Klavier- bzw. Orchesterbegleitung erklingt hierbei auf beiden Kanälen (ohne Violine) in Stereo-Qualität. Die Etüden wurden in sinnvolle Übe-Abschnitte unterteilt. Diese können Sie mit Hilfe der in der Solostimme angegebenen Track-Nummern auswählen. Weitere Erklärungen hierzu sowie die Namen der Künstler finden Sie auf der letzten Seite dieser Ausgabe; ausführlichere Informationen können Sie im Internet unter www.dowani.com nachlesen. Alle eingespielten Versionen wurden live aufgenommen.

Damit der Schritt von der CD zum Live-Erlebnis nicht fern ist, bieten wir allen Orchestern das komplette Aufführungsmaterial inklusive Partitur an.

Wir wünschen Ihnen viel Spaß beim Musizieren mit unseren *DOWANI 3 Tempi Play Along*-Ausgaben und hoffen, dass Ihre Musikalität und Ihr Fleiß Sie möglichst bald bis zur Konzertversion führen werden. Unser Ziel ist es, Ihnen durch Motivation, Freude und Spaß die notwendigen Voraussetzungen für effektives Üben zu schaffen.

Ihr DOWANI Team

I

G Major / Sol majeur / G-Dur

Ch. Dancla (1817 – 1907)

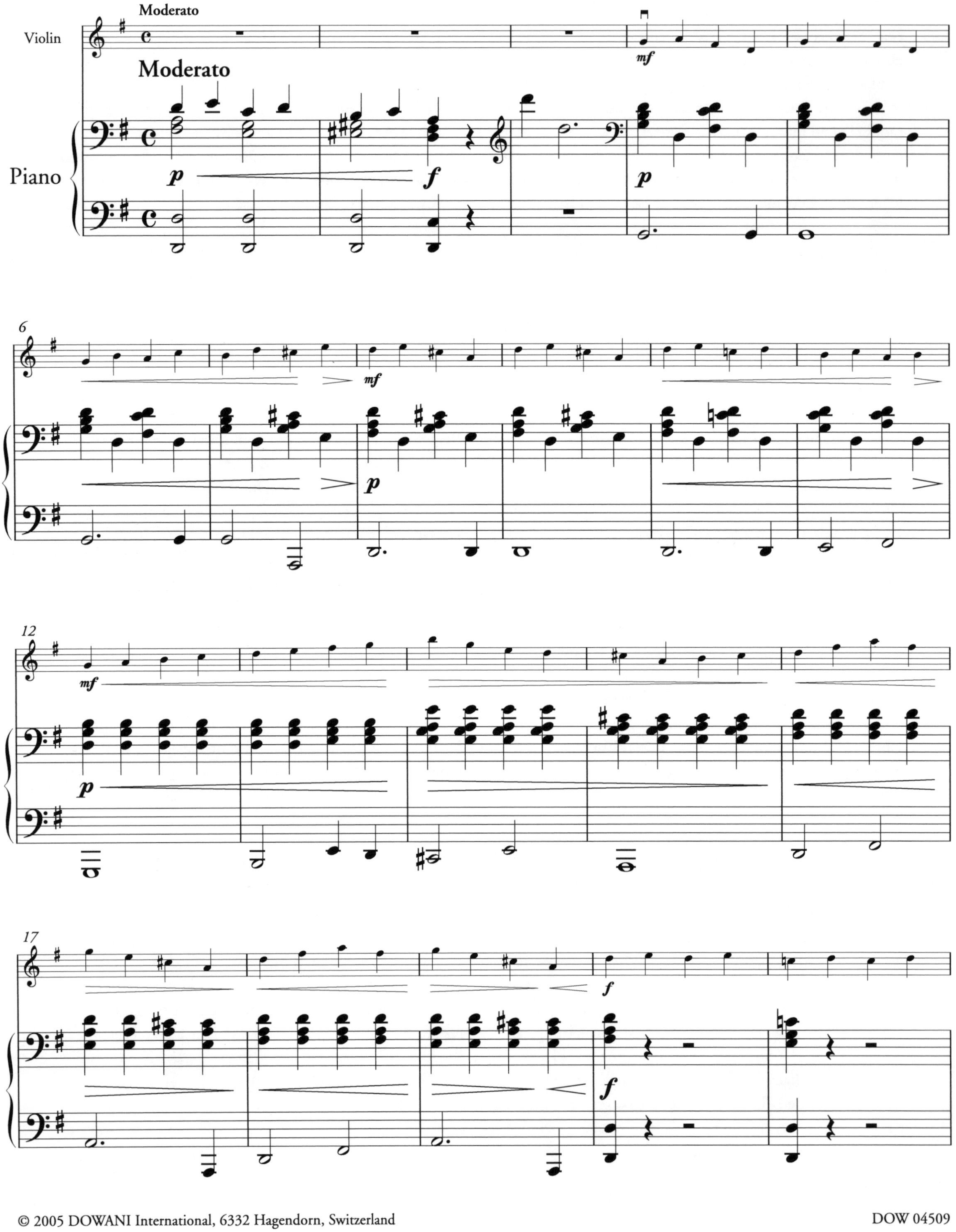

22
mf
mf
28
mf
mf
mf cresc.
mf cresc.
33
38
f decresc.
f decresc.
mf
mf
43

II

A Major / La majeur / A-Dur

Ch. Dancla (1817 – 1907)

23
cresc.
cresc.
28
f
mf
33
f
mf
38
f
mf
44
f
f

III

C Major / Ut majeur / C-Dur

H. E. Kayser (1815 – 1888)

19
mf
23
f
mf
28
cresc.
33
f
38

IV

A Major / La majeur / A-Dur

H. E. Kayser (1815 – 1888)

41
45
cresc.
cresc.
49
f
52
mf
55

17
21
26
31
36

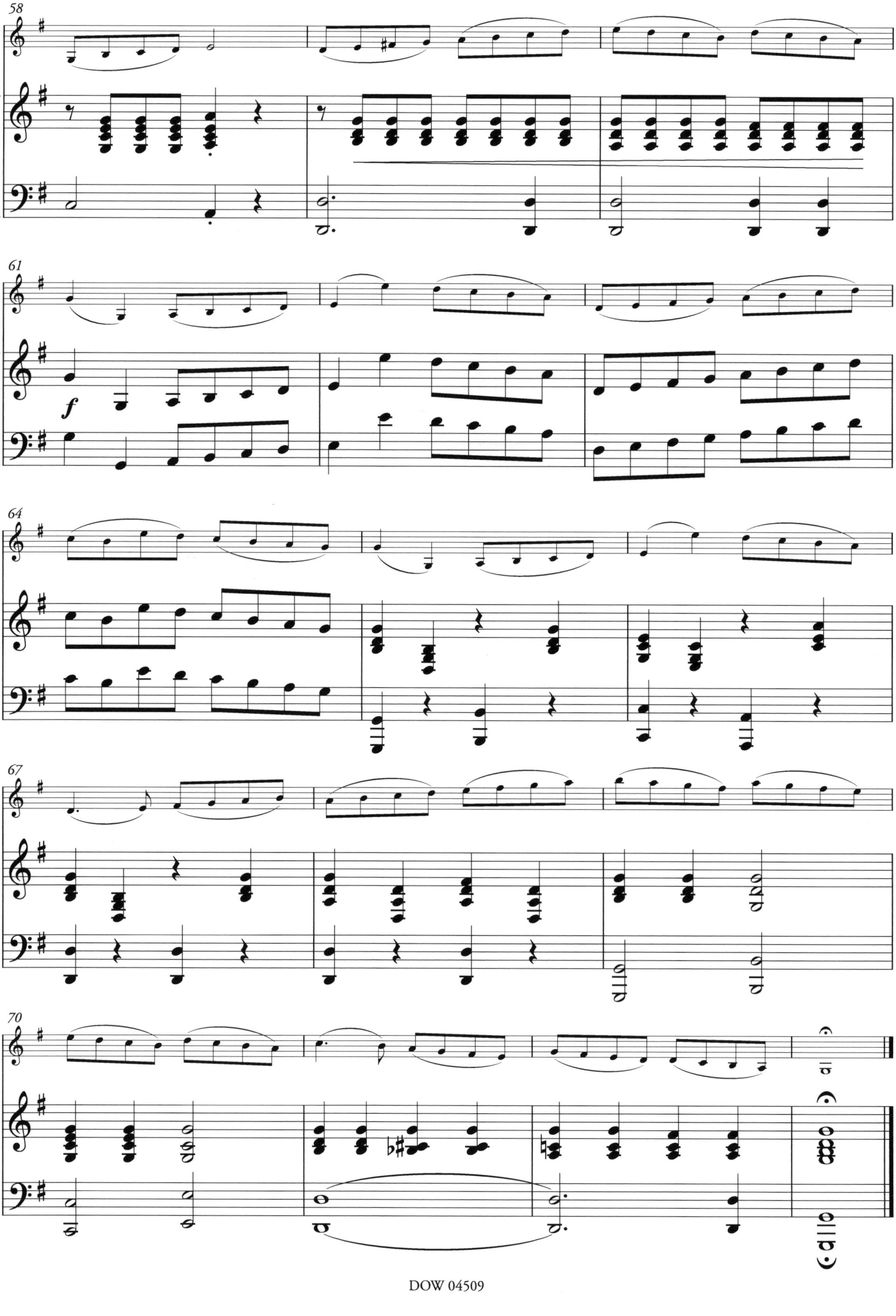
58
61
f
64
67
70

X

G Major / Sol majeur / G-Dur

F. Wohlfahrt (1833 – 1884), Op. 45 No. 3

mf
p
cresc.
cresc.
f
mf
f

ENGLISH

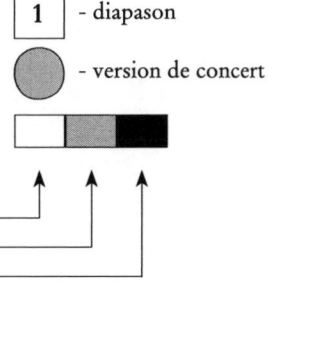

DOWANI CD:
- Track No. 1 — 1 - tuning notes
- Track numbers in circles — - concert version
- Track numbers in squares
  - slow Play Along Tempo
  - intermediate Play Along Tempo
  - original Play Along Tempo

- Additional tracks for longer movements or pieces
- **Double CD:** CD1 = A, CD2 = B
- **Concert version:** violin and orchestra
- **Slow tempo:** channel 1: violin solo; channel 2: piano accompaniment; middle position: both channels at the same volume
- **Intermediate tempo:** piano accompaniment only
- **Original tempo:** orchestra only

Please note that the recorded version of the piano accompaniment may diffe slightly from the sheet music. This is due to the spontaneous character of liv music making and the artistic freedom of the musicians. The original sheet music for the solo part is, of course, not affected.

FRANÇAIS

DOWANI CD :
- Plage N° 1 — 1 - diapason
- N° de plage dans un cercle — - version de concert
- N° de plage dans un rectangle
  - tempo lent play along
  - tempo moyen play along
  - tempo original play along

- Plages supplémentaires pour mouvements ou morceaux longs
- **Double CD :** CD1 = A, CD2 = B
- **Version de concert :** violon et orchestre
- **Tempo lent :** 1er canal : violon solo ; 2nd canal : accompagnement de piano ; au milieu : les deux canaux au même volume
- **Tempo moyen :** seulement l'accompagnement de piano
- **Tempo original :** seulement l'accompagnement d'orchestre

L'enregistrement de l'accompagnement de piano peut présenter quelques différences mineures par rapport au texte de la partition. Ceci est du à la liberté artistique des musiciens et résulte d'un jeu spontané et vivant, mais n'affecte, bien entendu, d'aucune manière la partie soliste.

DEUTSCH

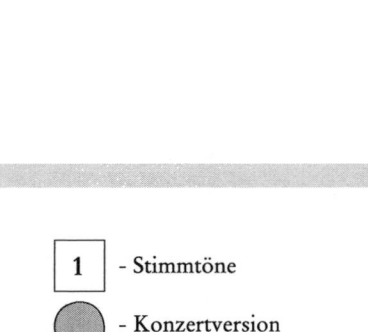

DOWANI CD:
- Track Nr. 1 — 1 - Stimmtöne
- Trackangabe im Kreis — - Konzertversion
- Trackangabe im Rechteck
  - langsames Play Along Tempo
  - mittleres Play Along Tempo
  - originales Play Along Tempo

- Zusätzliche Tracks bei längeren Sätzen oder Stücken
- **Doppel-CD:** CD1 = A, CD2 = B
- **Konzertversion:** Violine und Orchester
- **Langsames Tempo:** 1. Kanal: Violine solo; 2. Kanal: Klavierbegleitung; Mitte: beide Kanäle in gleicher Lautstärke
- **Mittleres Tempo:** nur Klavierbegleitung
- **Originaltempo:** nur Orchester

Die Klavierbegleitung auf der CD-Aufnahme kann gegenüber dem Notente kleine Abweichungen aufweisen. Dies geht in der Regel auf die künstlerisch Freiheit der Musiker und auf spontanes, lebendiges Musizieren zurück. Die Solostimme bleibt davon selbstverständlich unangetastet.

DOWANI - 3 Tempi Play Along is published by:
DOWANI International
A division of De Haske (International) AG
Postfach 60, CH-6332 Hagendorn
Switzerland
Phone: +41-(0)41-785 82 50 / Fax: +41-(0)41-785 82 58
Email: info@dowani.com
www.dowani.com

Recording & Digital Mastering: Pavel Lavrenenkov, Russia
Music Notation: Notensatz Thomas Metzinger, Germany
Design: Andreas Haselwanter, Austria

Concert Versio
Alexander Trostyansky, Violi
Russian Philharmonic Orchestra Moscov
Konstantin Krimets, Conducto

3 Tempi Accompanimen
Slow
Vitaly Junitsky, Pian

Intermediate
Vitaly Junitsky, Pian

Original
Russian Philharmonic Orchestra Moscov
Konstantin Krimets, Conducto

23
28
mf
34
39
cresc.
f
44
f

49
mf
53
57
cresc.
62
f
67
mf

71
76
80
85
f
90
f

V

G Major / Sol majeur / G-Dur

F. Wohlfahrt (1833 – 1884), Op. 45 No. 4

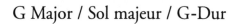

* Original: 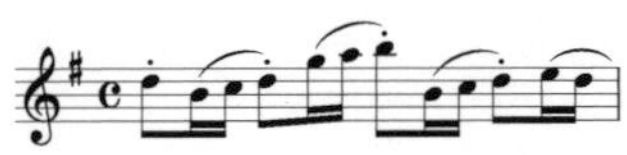

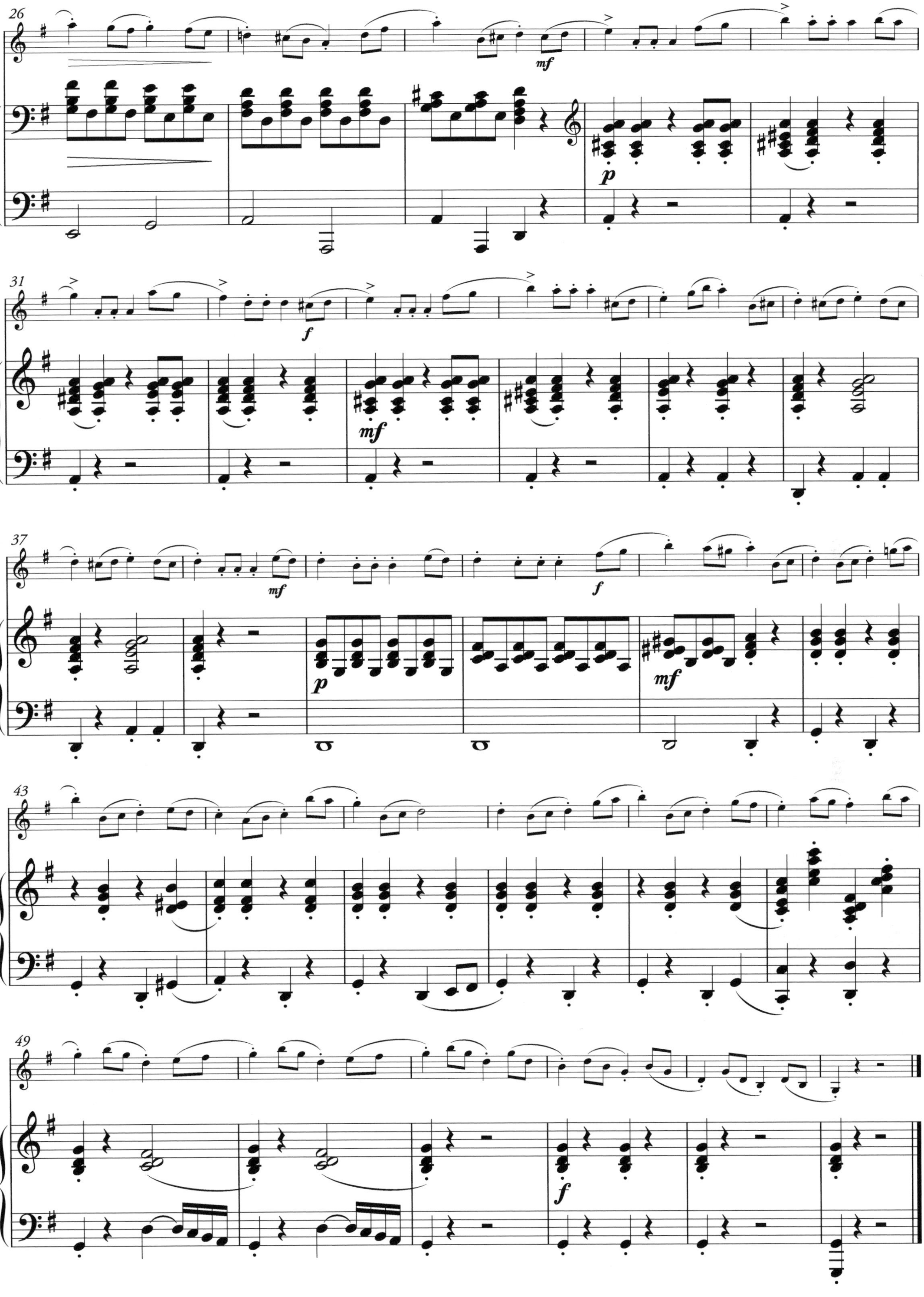

VI

D Major / Ré majeur / D-Dur

F. Wohlfahrt (1833 – 1884), Op. 45 No. 14

18
cresc.
22
26
f
30
f
mf
34
ff
ff

VII

D Major / Ré majeur / D-Dur

F. Wohlfahrt (1833 – 1884), Op. 45 No. 17

13
f
15
mf
18
cresc.
20
f

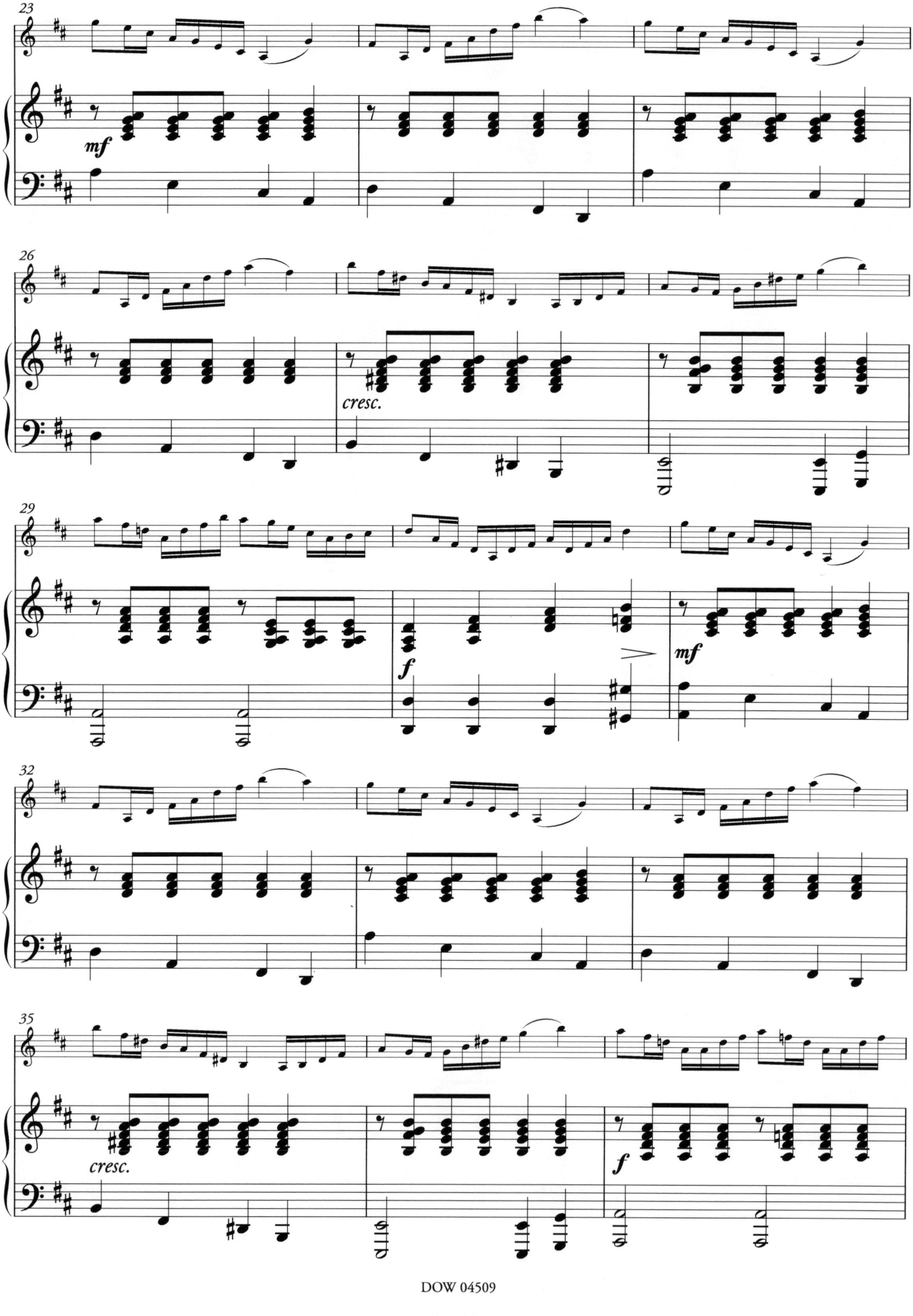
23
mf
26
cresc.
29
f
mf
32
35
cresc.
f

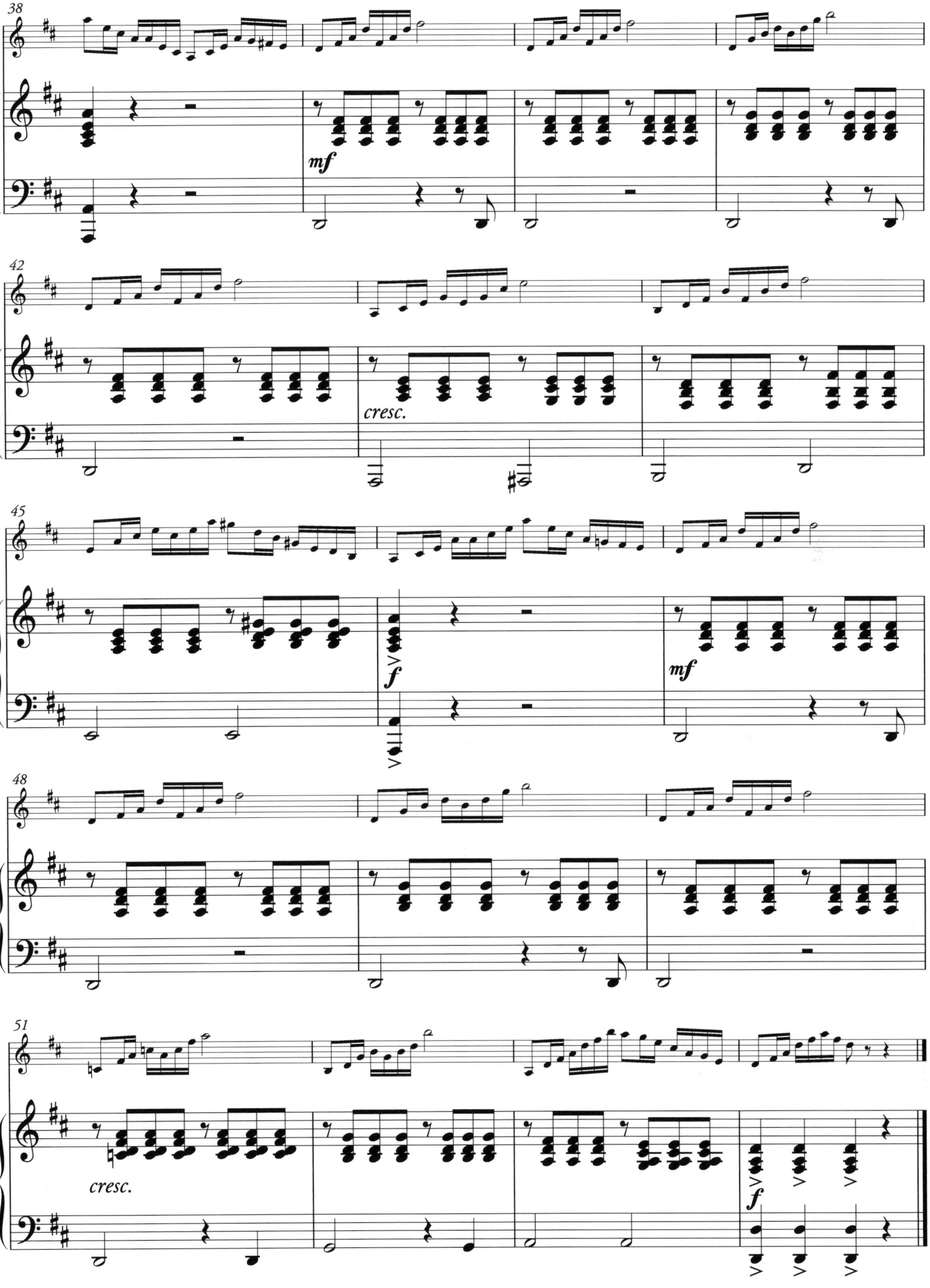

38
mf
42
cresc.
45
f
mf
48
51
cresc.
f

VIII

C Major / Ut majeur / C-Dur

H. Sitt (1850 – 1922), Op. 32 No. 1

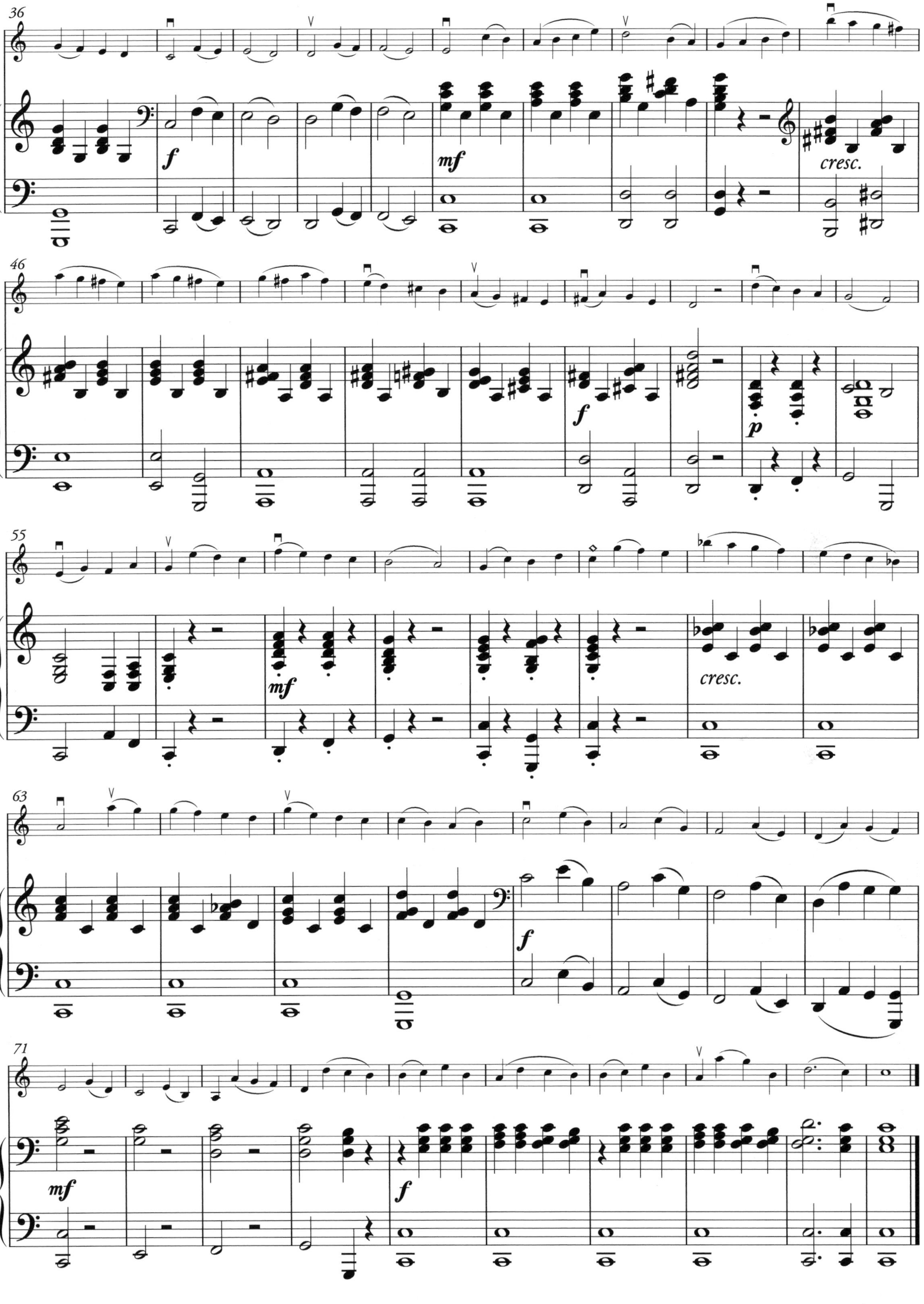
36
f
mf
cresc.
46
f
p
55
mf
cresc.
63
f
71
mf
f

IX

G Major / Sol majeur / G-Dur

H. Sitt (1850 – 1922), Op. 32 No. 2

EASY STUDIES Vol. I

by Ch. Dancla, H. E. Kayser, H. Sitt and F. Wohlfahrt
for Violin and Orchestra

(1st Position)

Violin / Violon / Violine

DOWANI International

Contents / Contenu / Inhalt

Violin

I (A2)

G Major / Sol majeur / G-Dur

Ch. Dancla (1817 – 1907)

II (A9)

A Major / La majeur / A-Dur

Ch. Dancla (1817 – 1907)

III (A16)

C Major / Ut majeur / C-Dur

A17 A19 A21

H. E. Kayser (1815 – 1888)

Allegro Moderato

IV (A23)

A Major / La majeur / A-Dur

H. E. Kayser (1815 – 1888)

V (A30)

G Major / Sol majeur / G-Dur

F. Wohlfahrt (1833 – 1884), Op. 45 No. 4

* Original: 

VI (B2)

D Major / Ré majeur / D-Dur

B3 B5 B7

F. Wohlfahrt (1833 – 1884), Op. 45 No. 14

VII B9

D Major / Ré majeur / D-Dur

F. Wohlfahrt (1833 – 1884), Op. 45 No. 17

28
31
34
37
40
43
46
49
52

VIII (B16)

C Major / Ut majeur / C-Dur

H. Sitt (1850 – 1922), Op. 32 No. 1

IX (B23)

G Major / Sol majeur / G-Dur

H. Sitt (1850 – 1922), Op. 32 No. 2

X (B30)

G Major / Sol majeur / G-Dur

F. Wohlfahrt (1833 – 1884), Op. 45 No. 3

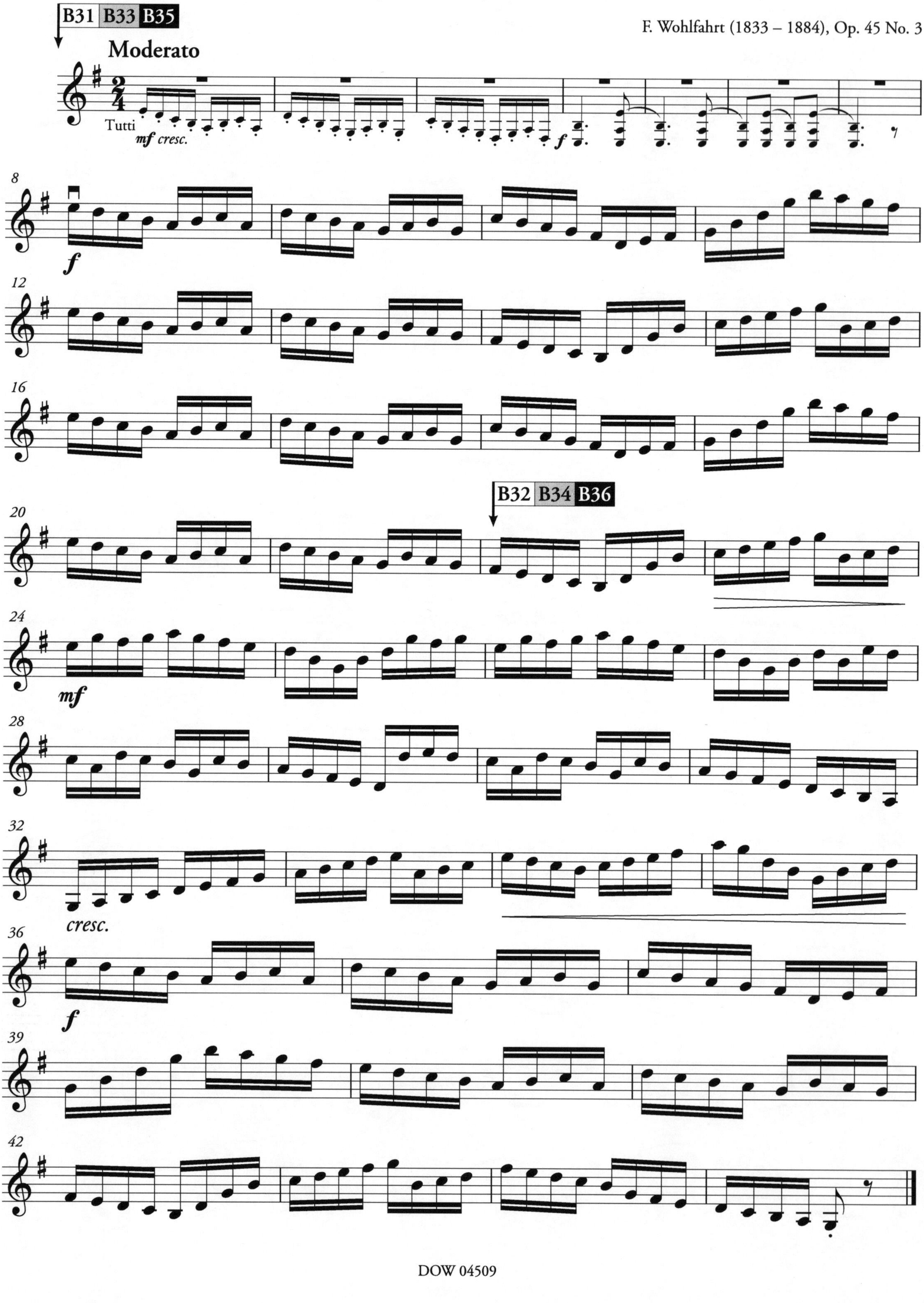